Word Power
Activities for Years 5 and 6

Terry Saunders

 David Fulton Publishers

David Fulton Publishers Ltd
The Chiswick Centre, 414 Chiswick High Road, London W4 5TF

www.fultonpublishers.co.uk

First published in Great Britain in 2004 by David Fulton Publishers
10 9 8 7 6 5 4 3 2 1

Note: The right of Terry Saunders to be identified as the author of this work has been asserted by her in accordance with the Copyright, Designs and Patents Act 1988.

David Fulton Publishers is a division of Granada Learning Limited, part of ITV plc.

Copyright © Terry Saunders 2004

British Library Cataloguing in Publication Data
A catalogue record for this book is available from the British Library.

ISBN 1-84312-142-5

Illustrations by Peter Stevenson
Typeset by FiSH Books, London
Printed and bound in Great Britain by Thanet Press

Contents

Preface

Unravelling the mysteries of our language is an intriguing, perplexing and exciting adventure. We discover clues, produce evidence, are led up blind alleys, unmask impostors, accept new theories, follow rules, break others, lose our nerve, grow in confidence and, occasionally, revel in our triumphs.

It seems impossible that from just 26 letters and about 40 sounds we can make up the thousands and thousands of words that we use every day to communicate our feelings, needs or opinions, our explanations, enquiries and expressions or our descriptions, demands and desires.

Once children begin to recognise the infinite variety and flexibility of our language they can begin to use it in very personal and subjective ways – to enhance their imagination, express their thoughts, clarify meaning, and to enjoy, entertain and amuse.

This second book in the series has been written to help children develop their initial excitement and fascination with words into a powerful and rewarding understanding of the way that we use language and the impact that it has on our daily lives.

I wanted to demonstrate its extraordinarily diverse make-up; the way that it is being constantly updated, rearranged and driven onwards by new words and words from other languages.

I tried to highlight its inconsistencies, ambiguities and complexities in spelling, pronunciation and meaning which lurk in almost every sentence, just waiting to catch us out.

And, most of all, I needed to show how rhyme and rhythm, humour and irony, magic and melody have helped to keep our language fast-moving, amusing and endlessly inventive.

Terry Saunders
January 2004

How to use this book

Word level

This *Word Power* series takes as its benchmark the vocabulary extension element from the *National Literacy Strategy*'s word level requirements. There are two books – *Word Power: Activities for Years 3 and 4* for seven- to nine-year-olds and *Word Power: Activities for Years 5 and 6* for nine- to eleven-year-olds – which explore all the major vocabulary elements at Key Stage 2. The series mirrors the Strategy's termly timetable with the activities running chronologically from Term 1 Year 3. In addition, it makes appropriate links with related requirements to ensure cohesion and relevance to children in each school year and to achieve the Strategy's important back-referencing and revisiting policy, introduced to increase and extend word skills as the children move through the key stage. It also brings together related Strategy elements as a way of reinforcing skills and confidence.

Helping teachers

Each chapter deals with a specific area of vocabulary and starts with teachers' guidelines outlining:

- *National Literacy Strategy* links
- links within the series
- definitions and information about the words, their importance and how we use them
- ideas for using the pupil activities
- suggestions for whole-class activities or challenges
- intriguing 'Did you knows?'

Stretching and challenging all children

The aim is always to stretch and challenge all children and to make them enthusiastic and confident wordsmiths. Throughout the series, the emphasis is on encouraging them to explore, and become familiar with, a range of different types of dictionaries and reference books – and, at the same time, to create personal and class word books, displays and dictionaries. In each chapter, the children's activities increase in levels of difficulty – building and dovetailing skills and knowledge – to cover varying abilities and ages. All the activities are photocopiable and have been designed to be used as worksheets in the classroom or as homework activities to reinforce teaching and learning.

Additional resources

At the back of the book, there is:

- an extra blank photocopiable worksheet so that children can write their own definitions of word groups or compile personal or class wordlists.
- an answers list. However, please note that, for some of the activities there are no right or wrong answers – the idea is to encourage children to choose and use their own words.

It is essential that children have access to a wide selection of dictionaries, including thesauruses and word reference books, for these activities.

Idioms, clichés and sayings – our language heritage

Guidelines for teachers

Introducing idioms, clichés and sayings

It is the everyday interpretations of our language – the use of idioms, sayings and expressions – that give it heart, character and warmth. However firm your grasp of tenses, clauses and syntax, the language will not come alive until you understand what cats and dogs have to do with heavy rain, why dressing to kill is more innocent than it appears and when you are most likely to see a bull in a china shop. Idioms are not meant to be taken literally. They are readily available, off-the-shelf, easy to use expressions – vocabulary's equivalent of ready meals – a common reference point in our dealings with situations, people, feelings or events. When they become so overused that they become meaningless, they become clichés.

In the classroom – starter activities

Children will find working with popular sayings exciting and reassuring, particularly when they realise that they already have a well-stocked supply stored in their own minds. Sort out the clichés from the idioms, explaining that clichés are often highly fashionable – the sayings of the moment. Compile an 'Idioms' Guide', in scrapbook form or on the classroom wall, arranged either alphabetically or themed, followed by a short explanation of what they mean. The children will know some of the meanings; encourage lively classroom debate about final explanations! Others will need to be researched using a phrase dictionary. Organise an assembly presentation using idioms about popular themes, or use them in a more serious way to spearhead an anti-bullying, environmental or health campaign in your school or community. Watch clips from television programmes – news, sports events, current affairs – and see how many idioms and clichés the children can spot.

Definition: What is an idiom?

An idiom is a common saying or phrase which most people understand and use, but which isn't meant to be taken literally.

Definition: What is a cliché?

A cliché is a phrase or expression which is overused and which then becomes tired and loses impact.

Why are they important to our written and spoken language

They:

- provide a common point of understanding
- act as a quick and easy expression of feelings or meaning
- add character and colour to our conversation or informal writing.

National Literacy Strategy – Years 5/6

The *National Literacy Strategy* features idiomatic phrases, clichés and common expressions in the requirements for Year 5, Term 1, revising work started on common expressions in Year 3, Term 3.

 DID YOU KNOW?
'Raining cats and dogs' came from northern mythology where witches in the form of cats rode on storms, making them the symbol of rain, and dogs, like wolves, were symbols of wind.

Every picture tells a story

What idioms do these drawings illustrate?

Animal crackers

Lots of idioms are about animals. Fill in the blanks with the names of the correct animals.

Taking the ....'s share

Like a .... to the slaughter

.... in your throat

Talking the hind legs off a ....

Weeping .... tears

Putting the .... among the ....

I smell a ....

Proud as a ....

2

Colour coded

Look at these idioms, which are all based on colour, and then choose one word which explains what they really mean and write it in the box.

Once in a blue moon.

In the pink.

Born with a silver spoon in his mouth.

It's a grey area.

It was a golden moment.

He was green with envy.

She saw red.

His mood was very black.

Idioms, clichés and sayings

Tell me a story

Write a short story based on one of the following idioms. Continue your story on a separate sheet if necessary.

Making a mountain out of a molehill.

Painting the town red.

Wonders will never cease.

....

....

....

....

....

....

....

....

....

4

Eye on the ball

Underline all of the idioms and clichés that you can find in this soccer report. Then choose three and fill in the boxes below to show what they mean.

The Blues are having to eat humble pie this afternoon after having the rug pulled out from under them in last week's head to head with Rangers. Of course, they will be pleased as punch if they win against United but Rome wasn't built in a day. Midfielder Wayne Brown has been read the riot act by captain Darren Smith about flying off the handle on the pitch – particularly after he went bananas when the ref booked him last week. Goalie Pete Jones commented: 'It's all in the lap of the gods but I'll be over the moon if we win today and sick as a parrot if we lose.'

Idiom/cliché	Meaning

5

What do they mean?

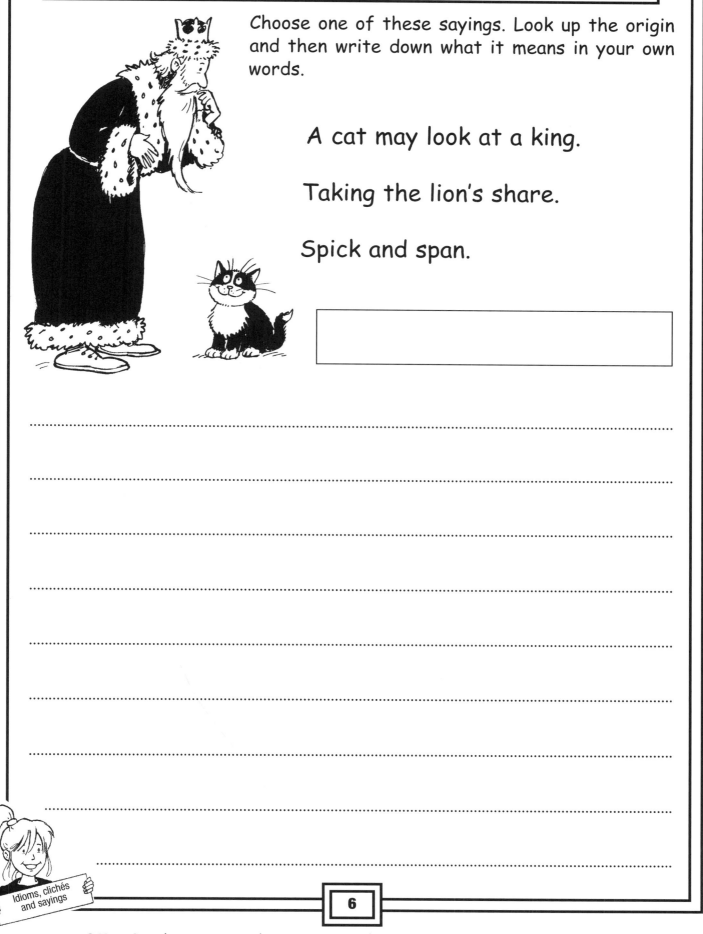

Choose one of these sayings. Look up the origin and then write down what it means in your own words.

A cat may look at a king.

Taking the lion's share.

Spick and span.

....
....
....
....
....
....
....
....

Idioms, clichés and sayings

6

Hold the front page

Write new headlines to replace these clichés:

Minister drops a clanger

Old lady taken to the cleaners

One in a million mum wins award

Tax bills go through the roof

Idioms, clichés and sayings

7

Round in circles

Choose a particular subject, such as weather, ships and sailing, animals. Write the theme in the centre of the large circle below and then fill in as many idioms and clichés about that theme as you can find (see example). Are there any that fit more than one theme?

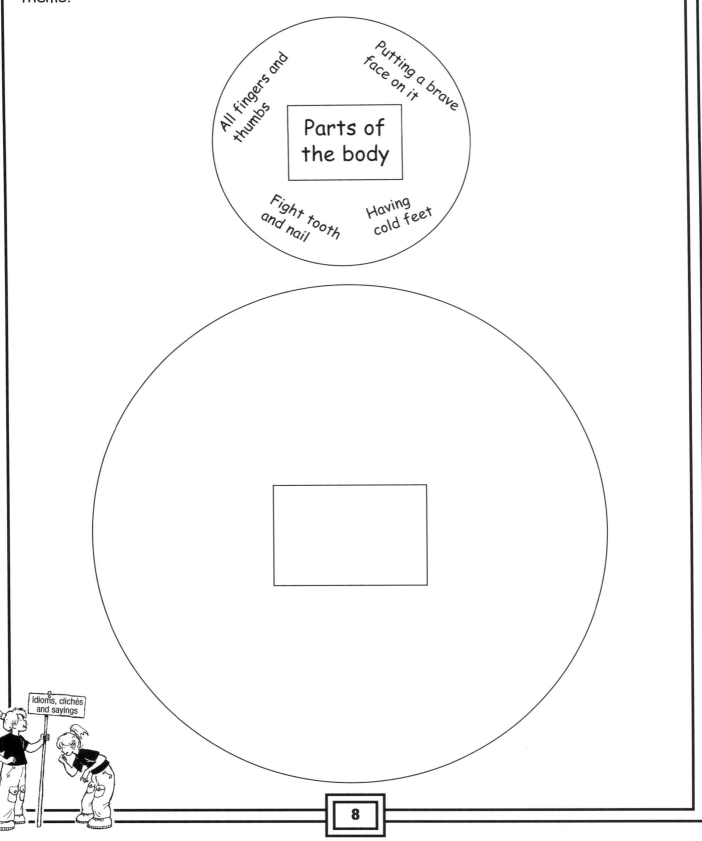

8

It's all in the game

Play this board game, which uses some well-known directional sayings, with your classmates and see who gets to the finish line first! All you need are some coloured counters and a dice.

START

1. Off to a flying start – go to 5

2. Put your best foot forward – go to 3

3. Don't look back – miss a turn

4. One step forwards, two steps back – go back to 3

5. Keep on track – miss a turn

6. Full steam ahead – go to 9

7. Up a blind alley – go back to 5

8. Slow and steady wins the race – go to 9

9. Make a beeline – go to 11

10. Lose your bearings – go back to 7

11. Sent to Coventry – go back to 5

12. Go the whole hog – go to Finish. You've won!

FINISH

9

Famous sayings

• • • Extension challenge • • •

1. William Shakespeare ☐

Look at these sayings and then match them to the famous person who said them.

a	I'd like to be a queen in people's hearts.
b	I have a dream...
c	In politics, if you want anything said, ask a man. If you want anything done, ask a woman.
d	All the world's a stage.
e	I belong to the whole world.
f	Genius is one per cent inspiration and ninety-nine per cent perspiration.

2. Martin Luther King ☐

3. Mother Teresa ☐

4. Thomas Edison ☐

5. Princess Diana ☐

6. Margaret Thatcher ☐

10

2 Onomatopoeia and alliteration – making an impact

Guidelines for teachers

Introducing onomatopoeia and alliteration

Learning to spell onomatopoeia – and other people's horror whenever you mention the word – are the only obstacles you should ever have to overcome when working with this very primitive and pleasurable element in our language. Children will grasp the impact that onomatopoeia can have on their writing and poetry quickly – and warm to the way it achieves particular effects, mood or atmosphere. Partnering onomatopoeia with alliteration will simply add to the excitement: enthusing and inspiring children to be creative and to experiment with, and explore, the important relationship between words and their sounds.

In the classroom – starter activities

Prepare for a noisy lesson as children get to grips with onomatopoeia! But first, challenge them to find ways to remember how to pronounce and spell such a long and complicated word. Once they realise what the word means, they will contribute to a class brainstorm with enthusiasm and zeal. Work with them to create a shared text in the classroom, based on a scene or situation full of atmosphere – such as a storm at sea or a Christmas pantomime – encouraging them to invent appropriate onomatopoeic words of their own. Set up a human orchestra with the children making the sounds of the instruments. Compile an onomatopoeic dictionary for the school library so that everyone can enjoy using such satisfying words.

Definition: What is onomatopoeia?

Onomatopoeia is a word which imitates or reflects the sound made by an object, person or animal.

Definition: What is alliteration?

Alliteration is a phrase or sentence where words next to, or near to, each other start with the same sounds.

Why are they important to our written and spoken language?

They:
- create impact, atmosphere and specific effects
- make the important link between words and sounds
- encourage exploration and experimentation with words and phrases.

National Literacy Strategy – Years 5/6

Collecting, using and inventing onomatopoeia is explored in Year 5, Term 2, reinforcing text level work of creating effects with onomatopoeia and alliteration in Year 3.

DID YOU KNOW?
The word onomatopoeia translates very simply into the Greek 'word making'. Would it make onomatopoeia more accessible if we stuck to that explanation?

Sounds good

Onomatopoeia and alliteration

Use the visual clues to help you work out these words which all take their names from their sounds.

snap   bash   crackle   boo   clang   bang   dazzle
slam   cuckoo   shoo   hiss   clash   tingle

13

Altogether now!

Many of the names we give to collections of animals sound just like the noise the animals make – for example, gaggle of geese or crash of rhinos. Have fun with collective nouns by making up some of your own. Which of these best match the animals shown here?

gurgle

shout

clatter

chatter

hiss

croak

_____ of _____

_____ of _____

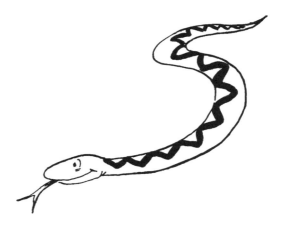

_____ of _____

_____ of _____

_____ of _____

_____ of _____

2

Tantalising tongue twisters

Alliteration is an important ingredient in tongue twisters – 'Round the rugged rocks the ragged rascal ran', or 'Peter Piper picked a peck of pickled pepper'.

Write some tongue twisters of your own – we've started you off with one complete example and the first words of two more. Try to say your tongue twisters as quickly as you can!

Five frisky fireflies found fourteen frowsy fossils floundering on a futon.

A wandering wallaby ....

....

Patsy Porter played ....

....

_____

My tongue twisters: ....

....

....

....

....

....

....

Onomatopoeia and alliteration

3

Mood swings

Combining alliteration with rhyme helps to make an impact when you are writing poetry. Build up a bank of descriptive phrases to help you with your poetry which cover different moods and pace, such as:

cold night: silent, solemn, starry skies

January: whining, whistling winter wind

tropical beach: jaunty, jet-propelled jellyfish.

Complete the chart below by choosing some key words of your own and the writing descriptive phrases for them. We have put in two words to start you off.

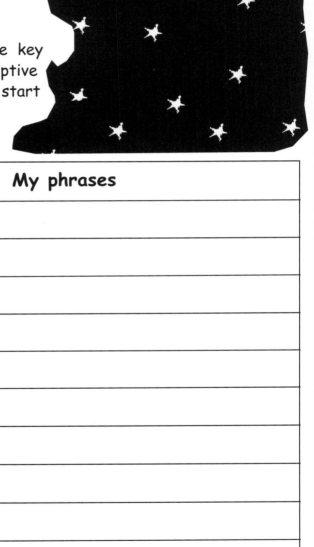

My key words	My phrases
Wolf	
desert	

4

© Terry Saunders (2004) *Word Power: Activities for Years 5 and 6*, David Fulton Publishers.

Creating atmosphere

• • • Extension challenge • • •

Look at this piece of text and underline all the examples of onomatopoeia and alliteration that you can find. Use two different coloured pens to distinguish between them.

Out of chaos

In the beginning there was only darkness – a still, silent darkness that filled the universe. The tiny cracks came slowly, carefully, cautiously, as if testing their potency and power. Then came the eruption, letting loose desperate, shattering shrieks as the rocks hurtled their way upwards, crashing and crunching together, splitting and slashing apart, banging and booming through the exploding firmament. From their core emerged flames, spitting and spewing molten lava in their wake, detonating all around like terrifying, gigantic firecrackers. As the waters of chaos surged forward into the void, it seemed as if the whole universe was bent on a terrible and tragic journey to destruction. Then, slowly, a piece of land rose out of the waters and on it stood Atum, the great creator god and saviour of the world. Atum lifted his arms and immediately started to calm the chaos.

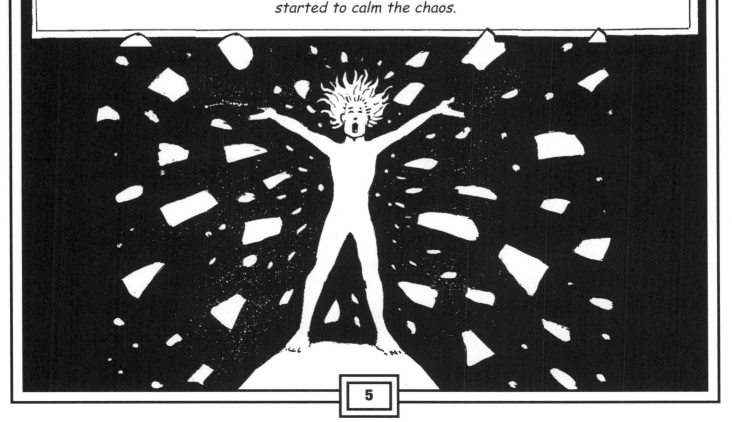

5

Technical and subject-specific vocabulary – subject words

Guidelines for teachers

Introducing subject-specific words

What is photosynthesis? Can you name a megalopolis? How would you describe a cartouche? These questions could easily come from a popular quiz programme – and underline our endless fascination with knowledge about a whole range of different subjects. Children, too, rise readily to the challenge presented by the subjects they encounter at Key Stage 2 – absorbing curious details and intriguing facts and learning to spell and define a variety of complex and intricate new words. Fortunately, much of what they learn will not only help them to understand specific subjects and increase and extend their word power but will also add a further important dimension to their knowledge of word making and building.

In the classroom – starter activities

Discuss with the children the way that many technical words have, and still are being, evolved or invented. Talk about the widespread use of prefixes, such as geo- or eco-, the building of compound words and adoption of foreign words and, last but not least, the origins of words which so often give clues to meaning. Using activities based on real-life situations – like some of those in this chapter – will highlight for the children the relevance and importance of these technical words. Create labelled posters or leaflets showing bird migration patterns, how trees help our atmosphere or the layout of a Roman fortress. Follow an archaeological dig, an environmental disaster or a satellite launch in the media or on the Internet.

Definition: What is technical language?

Technical language refers to the range of words which originate from, and are used, although not exclusively, in connection with a specific subject.

Why are technical and subject-specific words important to our written and spoken language?

They:

- enable us to access and understand important elements of a particular subject
- enable us to communicate our knowledge of, and opinions about, that subject
- add to our knowledge of word making and building.

National Literacy Strategy – Years 5/6

Collecting, spelling and defining technical words derived from work in other subjects is a requirement of the *National Literacy Strategy* for Year 5, Term 2 and links closely with non-fiction reading and writing throughout Key Stage 2.

DID YOU KNOW?

The Greek scientist Eratosthenes, working in Alexandria, measured the circumference of the world correctly to within seven kilometres in 200 BC by measuring shadows.

Archaeological finds

You have been asked to write the captions for some new artefacts for your local museum. Match up the correct caption cards and historical periods and then write your captions using at least one of the words in the word bank. Put in the headings before you start.

Greek vase – excavated, archaeologist, mythology, wine

Egyptian ankh – tomb, hieroglyphics, pharaoh, civilisation

Viking helmet – iron, warrior, armour, raiders, treasure

Ration books – World War II, rationing, shortages, coupons, the Blitz

1

The appliance of science

Look at the words at the bottom of the page and then using the clues see if you can fill in the correct scientific words.

Not drops, but rain ☐☐☐☐ ☐☐☐☐

It's certainly getting warmer ☐☐☐☐☐☐☐☐☐☐ ☐☐☐☐☐☐

A forceful attraction ☐☐☐☐☐☐☐☐

You'll have to wrap up warm ☐☐☐☐☐☐☐☐

Trees take this in... ☐☐☐☐☐☐ ☐☐☐☐☐☐☐

...and give this out ☐☐☐☐☐☐

Keeps our feet on the ground ☐☐☐☐☐☐☐

How green plants make food ☐☐☐☐☐☐☐☐☐☐☐☐☐☐

A state of water ☐☐☐☐☐☐☐☐☐☐☐☐

---

gravity   insulate   greenhouse   effect

magnetic   oxygen   photosynthesis

condensation   acid rain   carbon dioxide

Technical and subject-specific vocabulary

2

Global dimension

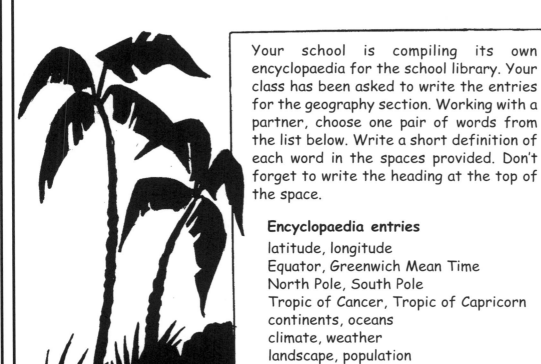

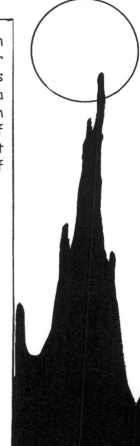

Your school is compiling its own encyclopaedia for the school library. Your class has been asked to write the entries for the geography section. Working with a partner, choose one pair of words from the list below. Write a short definition of each word in the spaces provided. Don't forget to write the heading at the top of the space.

Encyclopaedia entries

latitude, longitude
Equator, Greenwich Mean Time
North Pole, South Pole
Tropic of Cancer, Tropic of Capricorn
continents, oceans
climate, weather
landscape, population
earthquake, volcano
rivers, mountains
deserts, forests

3

Let's celebrate!

Each religion has its own series of festivals or celebrations each year. Can you match up the following events with the correct religion?

Festival of enlightenment ....

Easter...

Holi..

Sukkoth...

Ramadan ....

Diwali ....

Buddhist

Muslim

Sikh

Jewish

Christian

Technical and subject-specific vocabulary

Hindu

4

Critic's choice

Choose three reference books which give information on a subject you are studying at present. Investigate the different ways in which the books present the information you need. Is it easy to find your way around the book? Is the text written in a straightforward way?

Are there helpful illustrations or diagrams? Can you find all you need to know in one book?

Choose the best book and write a review of it to encourage other children to use it for their projects on the subject. Use one of the boxes for your notes and the other for your review.

Technical and subject-specific vocabulary

Notes	Review

5

Foreign words – around the world

Guidelines for teachers

Introducing foreign words

How many Portuguese, Mexican, Persian or Russian words do you know? If you think you've drawn a blank – think again. What about parasol, chocolate, caravan or mammoth? Add those to some of the better-known foreign words we already know about – pyjamas, bungalow and jungle (Indian), piano, umbrella and fiasco (Italian, or trash, janitor and hobo (American) – and the true extent of the influences that helped to form the English language becomes apparent. The basic Anglo-Saxon structure of our language flourished under a deluge of early influences – Greek and Latin, Scandinavian and French – and grew rich on the pickings of exploration, Empire and modern-day science and technology.

In the classroom – starter activities

Stick the largest map of the world that you can find to an even larger sheet of plain paper to use as a focal point for exploring foreign words in our language. Research words which have come into our language from particular countries, continents, cultures or civilisations and write them on pieces of card. Fix them to the plain paper surround, as near to the relevant places as possible, and pin a connecting piece of ribbon or tape between the words and the countries. Show off your knowledge of word origins by creating a quiz for the rest of the school – or for teachers and parents.

Definition: What are foreign words?

Foreign words are words that originate in foreign countries but have been absorbed into the basic Anglo-Saxon structure of our language.

Why are foreign words and phrases important to our written and spoken language?

They:

- have enhanced and enriched our language during the past 2,000 years
- have introduced variety and choice into our vocabulary
- have made our language one of the most versatile and accessible in the world.

National Literacy Strategy – Years 5/6

Foreign words feature in the *National Literacy Strategy* requirements for Year 5, Term 3. Make links with work on synonyms.

 DID YOU KNOW?
Although giraffes come from Africa, the word giraffe comes from Italy.

Long ago

The following groups of words came into our language long ago. Match them to the group of people who gave them to us – the Celts, Anglo-Saxons, Romans, Vikings.

Study the words carefully – they should give you some clues about their origins.

crag, down, crock, brock, lough

king, sword, knight, father, arm

street, wall, wine, shirt, cat

fell, beck, ford, husband, Thursday

When the Romans came

Foreign words

The Romans brought a new way of life to Britain – and gave many of our towns new names.

Can you find out the present-day names for these towns?

Londinium

Verulamium

Aqua Sulis

Venta Icenorum

Venta Siluram

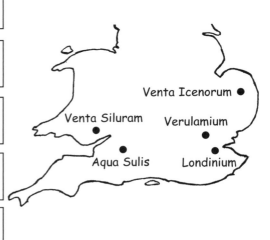

Venta Icenorum

Venta Siluram

Verulamium

Aqua Sulis

Londinium

The word venta meant market and aqua meant water. Fortress towns often included the word chester or cester. Using a map, try to find some examples of towns ending with this word.

Towns ending in chester or cester:

2

Meat here

The French have always had a reputation for fine food. Soon after the Normans invaded Britain, in 1066, the saying 'Saxon ox became Norman beef' became well known because the Normans called the meat by a different name to the animal it had come from. Fill in the Norman words for the meat from these animals which we still use today:

Ox	
Sheep	
Calf	
Pig	
Deer	

Which of these other foods did the Normans introduce? Put a tick or a cross in the box beside each food item.

Norman menu

cream	☐
spaghetti	☐
toast	☐
chocolate	☐
vinegar	☐
ketchup	☐
oranges	☐
bananas	☐
bacon	☐
turkey	☐

Foreign words

3

Double act

The Normans brought with them many new verbs which were absorbed into our language, giving us different words to choose from. What other words mean the same as the ones shown here? Use your thesaurus if you need some help.

Foreign words

aid...

commence...

conceal ....

defend...

desire ....

embrace ....

erode ....

purchase ....

retrieve..

satisfy..

4

Fruitful activity

It isn't just the variety of fruit we eat that comes from all over the world, the names we give them do, too. Can you match these fruit names to the country each comes from?

France

India

Mexico

Syria

Middle East

Arabia

Portugal

Mango	
Damson	
Tomato	
Lemon	
Apricot	
Artichoke	
Pomegranate	

5

© Terry Saunders (2004) *Word Power: Activities for Years 5 and 6*, David Fulton Publishers.

29

All creatures great and small

Our words for these animals come from other countries. When you have found out the correct country for each word, write it in the box underneath the drawing.

skunk

kangaroo

albatross

mongoose

sable

alligator

6

© Terry Saunders (2004) *Word Power: Activities for Years 5 and 6*, David Fulton Publishers.

What do they mean?

Lots of words and phrases which we use every day have been borrowed from other languages. Explain these phrases in your own words:

Latin

anno domini	
curriculum vitae	
status quo	

French

de luxe	
bon voyage	
nouvelle cuisine	

Italian

alfresco	
paparazzi	
al dente	

Spanish

Que sera sera	
fiesta	
aficionado	

Explorers

When European explorers returned home they brought with them all kinds of strange and wonderful objects, such as potatoes, tomatoes and tea. You are an explorer arriving home with one of these new objects. Choose your ojbect then complete this dialogue between yourself and your cook who is going to have to prepare the new food for you.

'Look what I've brought, cook, it's called ....'

'Well, that's a funny thing to be sure. What do I do with it?'

'It's easy; all you do is ....

....

....

....

....

....

....

8

India

There has been a close relationship between Britain and India for more than 200 years and many of the words that we now use every day originated in India.

These are just some of them. Write a definition of each word, as if you were writing an entry for an etymological dictionary:

Foreign words

veranda	
juggernaut	
jungle	
jodhpurs	
khaki	
bungalow	
shampoo	
chutney	
chintz	
dinghy	
dungarees	
curry	

9

Small world

These modern words have come to us from all over the world. Find out where they originated and then complete these sentences, filling in the names of the countries.

My friend's *karaoke* machine was made in ....

We travelled mostly on major *highways* when we drove across

....

I bought these postcards from the hotel *kiosk* when we were on

holiday in ....

Fancy going all the way to .... and finding *ketchup*

on the table.

Mum told me that lots of people in .... have a *sauna*

in their home.

Joe told me that the man who invented the word *robot* came from

....

It's as cold as .... today, I think I'd better wear my

fur-lined *anorak*.

Foreign
words

John wants to go *trekking* in ....

10

© Terry Saunders (2004) *Word Power: Activities for Years 5 and 6*, David Fulton Publishers.

Abbreviations – cutting it fine

Guidelines for teachers

Introducing abbreviations

Today's slick text-messaging techniques are a far cry from the old playground rhyme YYUR YYUB ICUR YY4ME. But words and phrases were being abbreviated long before mobile phones were invented. Our ancestors, as partial to short cuts as we are, were continually smoothing out awkward sounds in their everyday speech, cutting down on unnecessary phrases and amalgamating or abbreviating some of their most common words. It's human nature to experiment with word delivery and many abbreviated words start off as street language or slang – sarnie for sandwich, mash for mashed potato, spag bol for spaghetti bolognese – and slowly become an accepted part of our vocabulary. However, the explosion of abbreviations and acronyms in modern times, powered by science and technology and influenced by mass communication, is introducing us daily to a whole new vocabulary.

In the classroom – starter activities

Look at the different ways that words can be abbreviated – by leaving out letters and putting apostrophes in their place, by shortening words to make them more manageable or user-friendly, by forming a word from its acronym or by using letters for words. Write headings to cover each category on large sheets of paper and brainstorm examples for each sheet. Make links with everyday language and slang, with abbreviated foreign words and phrases, many of which are widely used every day, and with technical and scientific language.

Definition: What are abbreviations?

Abbreviations are words which have been shortened and which are now in common use.

Definition: What are Acronyms?

Acronyms are words that are made up of the first letter of each word in a title or phrase.

Why are abbreviations and acronyms important to our written and spoken language?

They:

- make our conversational language more manageable and user-friendly
- add to our language, helping it to develop in line with people's needs
- make scientific and technical language more accessible to ordinary people.

National Literacy Strategy – Years 5/6

Abbreviations and acronyms feature in the requirements for Year 5, Term 3, revisiting work from Year 3 and preparing the way for the study of new words in Year 6. Link with *National Literacy Strategy* requirements for everyday language and slang.

 DID YOU KNOW?

The word laser is an acronym for light amplification by stimulated emission of radiation.

Missing letters

Abbreviations

When we are talking we often abbreviate words or phrases because it helps to make our conversation flow. We put in an apostrophe to show the missing letters. Many of these abbreviations are also used in writing, particularly in informal writing or when we are writing dialogue. Write out the full meaning of these words or phrases:

I'd	
we've	
they're	
haven't	
doesn't	
can't	
won't	
shan't	
shouldn't've	
ne'er	
'twas	
pick'n'mix	
spick'n'span	
Hallowe'en	
five o'clock	

1

Short shrift

Many of the words we use today are simply shortened versions of longer ones. This happens when we use the words often – or when the full version is difficult or long and cumbersome. Can you give the original word that these shortened forms came from? Then use the box at the bottom of the page for any more shortened words that you use.

plane	
bike	
pram	
phone	
telly	
fridge	
car	
disco	
panto	
grotty	
hi-fi	

Shortened words I use

Abbreviations

2

© Terry Saunders (2004) *Word Power: Activities for Years 5 and 6*, David Fulton Publishers.

Cutting down

Abbreviations

When we are writing we often use formal, long-winded phrases or sentences instead of coming straight to the point. Match up the suitable single words to these long-winded phrases:

in spite of the fact that   near

at this moment in time   result

as a result of   despite

me, personally   until

end result   now

each and every   me

until such time as   each

in the vicinity of   because

3

© Terry Saunders (2004) *Word Power: Activities for Years 5 and 6*, David Fulton Publishers.

An initial look

All kinds of materials, places, countries, objects, groups of people and organisations are known by their initial letters or a shortened form of their name. What do these mean?

CD ....

MP ....

RSPCA ....

BBC ....

ITV ....

HGV ....

CID ....

DNA ....

GM (crops) ....

PC ....

COD ....

GP ....

Oxfam ....

Abbreviations

NATO ....

4

Sounds foreign

Some of our abbreviations come from foreign words. What everyday abbreviations do we use for these phrases? They are all Latin except the last one – which is French.

ante meridiem ....

post meridiem ....

et cetera ....

infra dignitatem ....

nota bene ....

post scriptum ....

répondez s'il vous plaît ....

5

6 New words which help our language grow – keeping up-to-date

Guidelines for teachers

Introducing new words

Every day of our lives, new words are being introduced into our language and, with modern methods of communication, many are quickly absorbed into our everyday speech and writing. Most are reinventions or rearrangements of other words – streetwise, edutainment, end-user – which have been compounded together in a fascinating and never-ending word game. There are scientific and technological terms, fashionable words promoted by show-business celebrities and street language and slang. There is also a craze for new verbs, readily manufactured to streamline our journey along the information highway. Working with new words will increase children's confidence and self-esteem as they witness the way their language is constantly being modified, developed and reinvented.

In the classroom – starter activities

Since many new words have come to us through computers, use the medium to set up a research project into new words. Use your school website, or set up a class file, to log and define new words when they arise. Encourage not just the children but other teachers, teaching assistants and parents to contribute to the research project and organise a working party to process the words on a daily or weekly basis. If you are using your website, invite other schools to take part. Organise words into groups or themes and use the information to study how new words arrive in our language and the extent to which they are being used. Are they just a passing fancy? Or will they be absorbed into the mainstream of our language? Use newspapers, magazines, children's comics and advertising material as resources as well as dictionaries.

Definition: What are new words?

New words are words that have been invented, redeveloped or rearranged to make new words or take on new meanings.

Why are new words important to our written and spoken language?

They:

- show us that language is alive and constantly changing, growing and developing
- enable us to use some of the elemental aspects of language to build new words
- ensure that ownership of the language remains with those who use it.

National Literacy Strategy – Years 5/6

Researching new words appears in requirements for Year 6, Term 1. Link with work on prefixes and suffixes and compound words throughout the key stage.

 DID YOU KNOW?
The most used new word today is dot.com.

On the road

Since the introduction of the motor car, a great many new words have been brought into our vocabulary. Write about a road journey using as many of these words as possible. Here are some examples to help you out:

cats' eyes	traffic lights	bottleneck
roundabout	carriageway	coned off
speedtrap	speedbumps	traffic calming
service station	slip road	hard shoulder

My journey

....

....

....

....

....

....

....

....

....

1

New beginnings

Find out the meaning of these prefixes which are currently being used to make new words and then match them up with the correct endings:

tele- geo- eco- mega- micro- cyber-

system, friendly, tourism

cosm, computer, wave

sphere, magnetism, meter

cafe, space, age

banking, photo, communication

star, bucks, watt

New words

2

Going online

Computers have brought a huge number of new words into our vocabulary – many of them are compound words, put together to make new words for the cyber-age. Can you match up the words correctly, putting together the pieces of the jigsaw?

base   ware   data

spread   type   web   down   web   site   on

line   text   active

load   ware   soft   hard

word

web   sheet   pass   inter   page

cam

New words

Let's verbalise

One aspect of modern language is the fashion for making new verbs. Complete these sentences using the new verbs in their modern sense.

The company is going to .... 200 jobs next year.

The Queen was .... with a silver bowl by the visiting head of state.

Now that the children have all left home, Mum and Dad decided to .... to a cottage.

Jack .... some research for his project on whales.

The new system of parking will .... on Friday morning.

The Government said that they will stop ....

Jane went shopping to .... her new outfit.

accessorise   downsize   downloaded

kick-in   axe

spinning   gifted

New words

4

Modern words

Work in groups or with a partner to investigate how many of these compound words would have been in use 100 years ago. Use encyclopaedias or the Internet to confirm your answers. Then add some compound words of your own that are more than 100 years old.

New words

hovercraft   toothpaste   newspaper   jumbo-jet

carseat   sheepskin   checkout   toyshop   supermarket

rollerskates   telephone   spinning-wheel   photocopy

Words that are more than 100 years old

Proverbs – words of wisdom

Guidelines for teachers

Introducing proverbs

Proverbs are the collective street wisdom of our civilisation. They offer advice, direction, warning, sympathy, criticism and cover almost every situation, event, type of person or creature. Many people see them as true reflections of our world, a way of making sense of our lives, or as a code to live by. This is because some of our proverbs originated in the Bible: 'The wise shall inherit glory: but shame shall be the promotion of fools' – and illustrate Solomon's pronouncements on wise men and fools; sentiments which have survived into many modern-day proverbs. Proverbs have become an integral part of our conversations, but those who take them seriously should beware. Many proverbs contradict each other – such as 'Absence makes the heart grow fonder' and 'Out of sight out of mind' – leaving us free to choose the one that best suits our particular purpose or situation.

In the classroom – starter activities

Discuss the difference between idioms and proverbs with the children. Reinforce the idea that proverbs offer wisdom and advice by setting up an 'advice centre' in the class. Divide the class into two and ask one group to come up with a list of 'problems' that need solving. The second group should find proverbs that provide the answer. For example: 'I forgot my granny's birthday. What should I do?' Answer: 'Send her a present now; better late than never.' You could also hold a proverb poetry writing competition where either the first or the last line is a proverb.

Definition: What are proverbs?

Proverbs are popular sayings which offer wisdom and advice.

Why are proverbs important to our written and spoken language?

They:

- highlight, and are a fine example of, our ancient literary history
- offer ready-made wisdom and advice for all situations
- show how words can be used concisely to make meaningful statements.

National Literacy Strategy – Years 5/6

Proverbs are a requirement for Year 6, Term 2. Make links with work on popular sayings Year 5, Term 1 and with work on synonyms and antonyms throughout the key stage.

 DID YOU KNOW?
The reason a pig's ear is featured in the proverb 'You can't make a silk purse out of a pig's ear' is because it was considered to be the most worthless piece of a pig after it was slaughtered.

Missing animals

Very many of our proverbs are about animals. Can you find the missing animals in these well-known proverbs?

Why keep a .... and bark yourself?

A .... never changes his spots.

.... always desert a sinking ship.

The early .... catches the worm.

Don't kill the golden .... that lays the golden eggs.

Don't break a .... on a wheel.

.... in mittens catch no mice.

Every .... likes to hear himself bray.

An .... never forgets.

Every flock has a black ....

He who rides the .... is afraid to dismount.

Here's the weather forecast

Write a weather forecast for your area based on one of these popular weather proverbs:

It's an ill wind that blows no one any good.

Make hay while the sun shines.

Rain before seven, dry before eleven.

One swallow doesn't make a summer.

After the storm comes the calm.

Weather forecast

....

....

....

....

....

....

....

....

Proverbs

2

Means the same

There are lots of proverbs which can be used to say the same thing. In the list below all the examples share the same meaning. See if you can complete the proverbs and then write in the box below what you think they mean.

You can't make a silk purse ....

You can't make bricks ....

You can't make an omelette...

You can't get a quart..

You can't get blood...

All these proverbs mean:

Proverbs

3

Is that so?

Many proverbs make firm statements about emotions and senses. Can you match up the beginnings and ends of these proverbs? Then write a synonym for each of the endings.

Synonym

Small is ....

Time is ....

Ignorance is ....

Love is ....

Enough is ....

Silence is ....

Revenge is ....

sweet   beautiful   blind

golden

money

enough   bliss

Proverbs

4

Hitting the headlines

• • • Extension challenge • • •

Choose one of these proverbs and write a newspaper story on your word processor based on its meaning. The ideas written underneath are just suggestions. You can use them if you want to, or you can try to think up a storyline of your own which matches the meaning of the proverb.

A bad workman blames his tools

new bridge collapses at opening ceremony

Great oaks from little acorns grow

children who planted new forest win environmental award

Home is where the heart is

cat whose owners moved 100 miles away walks to new home

Honesty is the best policy

bungling burglar gets caught in cat flap

5

Proverbs

Metaphors and similes – sounds like...

Guidelines for teachers

Introducing metaphors and similes

Metaphors and similes inject magic and imagination in our language. We can turn people, feelings, happenings into something else, or devise fascinating and intriguing comparisons between even the most unlikely objects. Metaphors can be liberating and exciting when used innovatively but they can also reduce our words to the predictable and humdrum. Avoid overused lacklustre metaphors, *fly in the ointment*, and similes, *flat as a pancake*. Worst of all, are the mixed metaphors beloved by politicians and celebrities – such as *I've kept my eye on the ball while exploring every avenue*.

In the classroom – starter activities

Discuss the differences between metaphors and similes with the children – explaining that with metaphors we say something *is* something else, while with similes we say it is *like* something else. Create some illustrated class posters. For similes, put a key word in the centre, for example, sun, mountain, cave, bridge, and encourage the children to surround the word with appropriate similes. For metaphors, create characters with speech bubbles containing metaphors and ask the children to add meanings.

Definition: What are metaphors?

Metaphors are sayings or phrases where something is described as something else.

Definition: What are similes?

Similes are sayings or phrases where something is likened to something else.

Why are metaphors and similes important to our written and spoken language?

They:
- give scope for imaginative speaking and writing
- enable ideas or explanations to be communicated easily and succinctly
- enable us to experiment with language.

National Literacy Strategy – Years 5/6

Metaphors and similes appear in Year 5, Term 1 and finally, along with new words and sayings, in the requirements for Year 6, Term 3 under the heading 'Experimenting with language'. Link throughout Key Stage 2 with different kinds of sayings and descriptive writing.

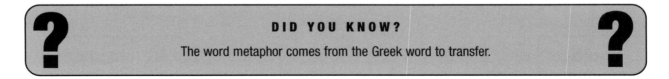

DID YOU KNOW?
The word metaphor comes from the Greek word to transfer.

As easy as falling off a log

Metaphors and similes

We regularly use a range of ready-made similes in our descriptions. Match up these popular similes into well-known sayings:

as light as	two short planks
as smooth as	night
as black as	nails
as solid as	a feather
as white as	the hills
as hard as	a rake
as dry as	silk
as thin as	a rock
as thick as	a bone
as old as	a sheet

Setting the scene

Create similes for all of these different scenes to use in your story writing:

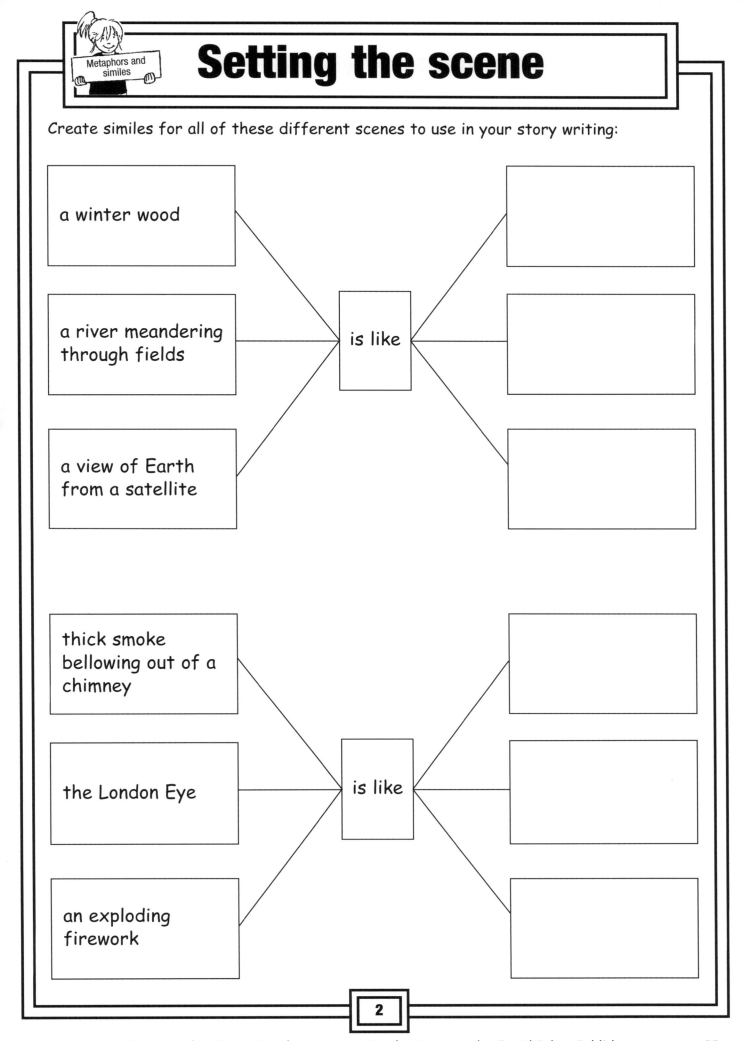

a winter wood

a river meandering through fields

a view of Earth from a satellite

is like

thick smoke bellowing out of a chimney

the London Eye

an exploding firework

is like

2

Metaphorically speaking

You will almost certainly have heard these well-known metaphors many times – you may even have used them yourself. What do they actually mean?

He had the world in his hands.

....

....

She explored every avenue.

....

....

It was a bolt from the blue.

....

....

They were over the moon.

....

....

The sky fell in.

....

....

He walked straight into a storm.

....

....

Metaphors and similes

3

© Terry Saunders (2004) *Word Power: Activities for Years 5 and 6*, David Fulton Publishers.

Not what they seem

Some metaphors are also idioms. See if you can fill in the verb at the beginning of these popular metaphors, for example: *chew* the cud or *play* with fire.

	castles in the air
	the candle at both ends
	off more than you can chew
	on the other side of your face
	the gun
	your words
	from the ashes
	wolf
	tooth and nail
	the hatchet

Metaphors and similes

4

Only human

• • • Extension challenge • • •

In some metaphors, human actions, emotions or characteristics are given to non-human objects or ideas, such as the darkening sky *embraced* the whole landscape.

What human actions do these illustrations suggest to you?

waves .... as they hit the rocks

wind .... through the trees

flowers .... in the breeze

sun .... down on us

bridge .... over the river

stream .... as it flows over pebbles

5

Puns, riddles and crosswords – wordplay

Guidelines for teachers

Introducing wordplay

Our language would surely not have gone through so many changes and developments if playing with words were not such great fun. Throughout history, human beings have indulged their fascination with words, not just as a necessity for communication, but also for enjoyment, amusement and challenge. The Greeks and Romans loved puns and riddles and used them profusely. Shakespeare excelled at puns; Lewis Carroll was famous for his love of word games; and crosswords, not yet a century old, are now reported to be the most popular word puzzles in the world. Once you have aroused children's interest in the sheer fun of playing around with words, you will have converted them to a love of language for the rest of their lives.

In the classroom – starter activities

Take time to plan a word games' day with plenty of different activities for the children to try. Keep up the momentum by inviting them to make up games of their own, once they understand the way games work. Include opportunities for joke-telling sessions – some of the most basic children's jokes rely on clever wordplay – which will help to build atmosphere and confidence. Devise a wordplay presentation, using the material you have uncovered, to show others in the school or community just how much fun words can bring.

Definition: What is meant by wordplay?

Wordplay means playing with words and word patterns in a way that entertains and amuses.

Why is wordplay important to our written and spoken language?

It is important because it:

- brings humour, wit and amusement to our language
- brings an understanding of the flexibility and range of language
- challenges and tests our knowledge of words and their meaning.

 DID YOU KNOW?
The Romans held riddle competitions at their annual feast of Saturnalia.

Riddle-me-re

Riddles have been one of the most popular forms of wordplay since before Roman times. Can you work out this riddle which is based on the alphabet? The answer tells you what this book is about. Then try to create some riddles of your own. Start with shorter ones, perhaps based on some jokes you know.

My first is for victory, battles we've won

My second's a circle, as round as the sun.

My third stands for vision, what can you see?

My fourth's the first letter, comes before B.

My fifth leaves a sting as it buzzes around

My sixth isn't me but it's you I'll be bound.

My seventh's a right angle, Spanish for *the*

My eighth is one more first, used so frequently.

My ninth's number eighteen, a consonant strong

My last is a question – please don't get it wrong.

My whole stands for words – a gift we should treasure

May I always be there for you, bringing you pleasure.

Answer

My riddles

Speaking of puns

Everyone groans at puns, but take no notice! They can show some very clever wordplay. Add the appropriate adverbs to the end of these phrases to make a pun, for example: 'I've been to the North Pole,' said Joe (coldly).

'The pyramids are in the desert,' Maria pointed out...

'The dogs will pull the sledge,' explained Harvinder...

'Let's switch the torch on,' suggested Will..

'Don't make such a noise,' instructed Millie ....

'I'll take you up in a hot air balloon,' offered James...

'When I grow up I want to compile dictionaries,' announced Jane...

'I've got to leave in seven days,' moaned Dan...

'I never win at darts,' mumbled Manjit...

airily   soundly   weakly

meaningfully   aimlessly

huskily

Puns, riddles
and crosswords

drily   lightly

2

© Terry Saunders (2004) *Word Power: Activities for Years 5 and 6*, David Fulton Publishers.

Name that pun

Puns based on names have always been popular – and one of the best-known ways of using this form of pun-making is using fictitious book titles and authors. See if you can match these authors to their books. Then create some of your own.

Travelling Light

Millie Pede   Stormy Weather

Clifftop Tragedy   Eileen Dover

Great Floods of our Time   Teresa Green

Prison Memoirs   The Rites of Spring

Terry Bull   Gail Force   Ivor Bucket

Puns, riddles and crosswords

Title

Author

....

....

....

....

....

....

....

3

Rebus

A rebus is a way of writing in code that uses numbers, letters and drawings to hide a message. See if you can work out what Billy is writing to his friend, Heidi. Then start to compile a Rebus alphabet of your own – we have given you some ideas to start you off. You will find that your text-messaging skills come in very handy!

Rebus alphabet	
THNQ = Thank you NE = any H8 = hate XQQ = excuse :-) = happy	:-(= sad . = stop up = high up (up written at the top of the line = high) low d = load (d written underneath the line = low)

THNQ 4 .ing 2 walk 2 me 2 day.
H8 having NE 2 C more of u.
U make me :-). H UR having an
X CD player 4 .
? could B NICR. XQQ .

Puns, riddles and crosswords

4

© Terry Saunders (2004) *Word Power: Activities for Years 5 and 6*, David Fulton Publishers.

63

Acrostic

An acrostic is a puzzle where the first letter in each line spells out a name or a word. These acrostics are about ancient Egypt. Write an acrostic for the words given here – the first one is completed for you.

NILE
Nefertiti, Queen so fair
Isis, searching everywhere
Luxor, where the tombs were found
Egypt's wonders still abound

M..

U..

M..

M..

Y..

P..

Y..

R..

A..

M..

I..

D..

5

Word squares

Word squares can be as big or as small as you want them to be. Use the clues to work out these word squares, then try to make some word squares of your own using the frames at the bottom of the page.

Blind as a ....

Sharp as an ....

Five and five make ....

B	A	T

Wild Scottish hills

Something dug up from the past

A saying: .... and kicking

The opposite of taken

A landscape or place of dramatic action

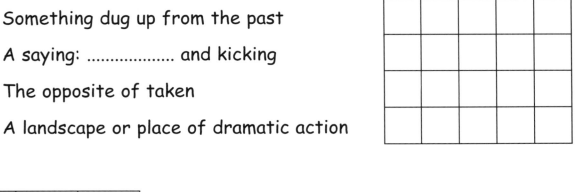

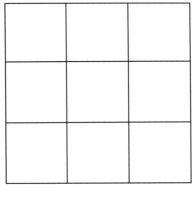

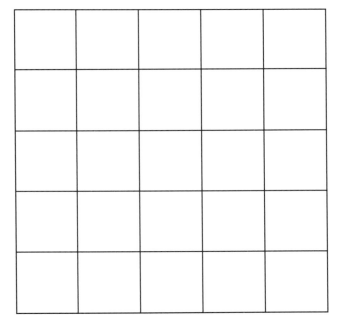

Puns, riddles and crosswords

Letter games

Names are popular for letter games. Take the letters and rearrange them into as many words as possible. See how many words you can make from the names below. Some examples are given to start you off. You can either take the letters from anywhere in the name or use only letters that are next to each other. Then write your own name in the box at the bottom of the page and see how many words you can make.

WILLIAM SHAKESPEARE

Letters from anywhere:

wheels

mask

small

Letters next to each other:

pea

ill

Liam

ALEXANDER THE GREAT

Letters from anywhere:

Letters next to each other:

WINSTON CHURCHILL

Letters from anywhere:

Letters next to each other:

My name:

Puns, riddles and crosswords

7

Palindromes

Palindromes are words or phrases which read the same backwards and forwards, for example:

Was it a cat i saw
Able was I ere I saw Elba

See if you can find any more palindrome words or phrases in reference books. Then look at these clues to help you begin to compile a list of words that are palindromes. Can you think of any more?

Short for mother

Short for father

Twelve o'clock

...goes the weasel

Seed found in oranges

Baby dog

Knights of old performed this

Boy's name, short for Robert

Girl's name, from the Bible, starts with H

Palindromes I have discovered:

Puns, riddles and crosswords

8

Pangrams

Pangrams are phrases which use all the letters of the alphabet. The most famous example is:

The quick brown fox jumps over the lazy dog.

People learning to type are encouraged to practise this pangram. Another is:

Quick waxy bugs jump the frozen veldt.

Pangrams have always been one of the most challenging word games. See how many phrases you can write using as many letters of the alphabet as you can. It doesn't have to be all of them, but try to use some of the more difficult letters – z, x, q. Work out words containing these letters first and then incorporate them into your sentence.

a b c d e f g h i j k l m n o p q r s t u v w x y z

....

....

....

....

....

....

9

Crossword clues

• • • **Extension challenge** • • •

It is incredible to think that it is less than a century ago that crosswords were invented. They are now the most popular word game in the world – responsible for putting a dictionary in almost every household! The challenge, of course, is in the clues. Write crossword clues for the following words about language and then choose two of your favourites. Write crossword clues for them in the boxes at the bottom of the page:

Puns, riddles and crosswords

metaphor	cliché	synonym	antonym
homonym	acronym	prefix	suffix
mnemonic	simile	apostrophe	idiom
clerihew	proverb	alliteration	kenning
epitaph	rhyme	riddle	abbreviation

_____

_____

Answers for activities for Years 5 and 6

Idioms, clichés and sayings

Every picture tells a story. pulling the wool over your eyes; easy as falling off a log; a pretty kettle of fish; money for old rope; sticking out like a sore thumb.

Animal crackers. lion, lamb, frog, donkey, crocodile, cat, pigeons, rat, peacock.

Colour coded. occasionally, healthy, rich, uncertain, successful, jealous, angry, depressed.

Tell me a story. Writing activity.

Eye on the ball. eat humble pie (apologise); rug pulled out from under them (lose out); head to head (confrontation); pleased as punch (delighted); Rome wasn't built in a day (some complicated tasks cannot be completed quickly); read the riot act (told off); flying off the handle (losing your temper); went bananas (went berserk); in the lap of the gods (in the hands of destiny); over the moon (excited); sick as a parrot (devastated).

What do they mean? even the lowliest have rights; the biggest share; neat and tidy.

Hold the front page. Children's choice.

Round in circles. Children's choice.

It's all in the game. Children's game.

Famous sayings. 5a I'd like to be a queen in people's hearts (Princess Diana); 2b I have a dream... (Martin Luther King); 6c In politics, if you want anything said, ask a man. If you want anything done, ask a woman (Margaret Thatcher); 1d All the world's a stage (William Shakespeare); 3e I belong to the whole world (Mother Teresa); 4f Genius is one per cent inspiration and ninety-nine per cent perspiration (Thomas Edison).

Onomatopoeia and alliteration

Sounds good. bang, clash, clang, hiss, slam, bash, shoo, boo, dazzle, crackle, snap, cuckoo.

Altogether now! Suggestions:

a gurgle of goldfish; a shout of apes; a clatter of horses; a chatter of monkeys; a hiss of snakes; a croak of toads.

Tantalising tongue twisters. Children's choice.

Mood swings. Children's choice.

Creating atmosphere. *Alliteration:* still, silent; carefully, cautiously; potency and power; letting loose; shattering shrieks; crashing and crunching; splitting and slashing; banging and booming; spitting and spewing; terrible and tragic; great creator god; calm the chaos.

Onomatopoeia: cracks, eruption, hurtled, crashing, crunching, splitting, slashing, banging, booming, exploding, spitting, spewing, firecrackers, surged.

Technical and subject-specific vocabulary

Archaeological finds. Children's choice.

The appliance of science. acid rain, greenhouse effect, magnetic, insulate, carbon dioxide, oxygen, gravity, photosynthesis, condensation.

Global dimension. Children's choice.

Let's celebrate! Buddhist, Christian, Hindu, Jewish, Muslim, Sikh.

Critic's choice. Writing activity.

Foreign words

Long ago. Celts, Anglo-Saxons, Romans, Vikings.

When the Romans came. London, St Albans, Bath, Norwich, Caerwent.
Suggestions: Cirencester, Colchester, Chichester, Gloucester, Woodchester, Silchester.

Meat here. beef, lamb, veal, pork, venison; cream, toast, vinegar, oranges, bacon.

Double act. help, begin, hide, guard, want, hug, destroy, buy, find, please.

Fruitful activity. India, Syria, Mexico, Middle East, Portugal, Arabia, France.

All creatures great and small. skunk (North America), kangaroo (Australia), albatross (Portugal), mongoose (India), sable (Russia), alligator (Spain).

What do they mean? Latin: AD – in the year of our Lord; CV – account of education and career to date; as it stands. French: superior quality; have a good trip; new style of cooking. Italian: in the open air; tabloid newspaper photographers; to the tooth (still firm). Spanish: what will be, will be; celebration; well-informed enthusiast of sport or hobby.

Explorers. Writing activity.

India. As dictionary definition.

Small world. Japan, America, Turkey, China, Finland, Czechoslovakia, Greenland, South Africa.

Abbreviations

Missing letters. I would, we have, they are, have not, does not, cannot, will not, shall not, should not have, never, it was, pick and mix, spick and span, All Hallows evening, five of the clock.

Short shrift. aeroplane, bicycle, perambulator, telephone, television, refrigerator, motor car, discotheque, pantomime, grotesque, high fidelity.

Cutting down. despite, now, because, me, result, each, until, near.

An initial look. compact disc, Member of Parliament, Royal Society for the Prevention of Cruelty to Animals, British Broadcasting Corporation, Independent Television, heavy goods vehicle, Criminal Investigation Department, deoxyribonucleic acid, genetically modified, personal computer or politically correct, cash on delivery, general practitioner, Oxford Committee for Famine Relief, North Atlantic Treaty Organisation.

Sounds foreign. a.m., p.m., etc., *infra dig.*, NB, PS, RSVP.

New words

On the road. Writing activity.

New beginnings. ecosystem, eco-friendly, eco-tourism; microcosm, microcomputer, microwave; geosphere, geomagnetism, geometer; cybercafe, cyberspace, cyber-age; telebanking, telephoto, telecommunication; megastar, megabucks, megawatt.

Going online. download, online, text-type, website, webpage, webcam, database, spreadsheet, software, hardware, interactive, password.

Let's verbalise. axe, gifted, downsize, downloaded, kick-in, spinning, accessorise.

Modern words. toyshop, toothpaste, newspaper, rollerskates, sheepskin, spinning-wheel.

Proverbs

Missing animals. dog, leopard, rats, bird, goose, butterfly, cats, ass, elephant, sheep, tiger.

Here's the weather forecast. Writing activity.

Means the same. You can't make a silk purse out of a pig's ear. You can't make bricks without straw. You can't make an omelette without breaking eggs. You can't get a quart into a pint pot. You can't get blood out of a stone. What you are attempting to do is impossible.

Is that so? beautiful, money, bliss, blind, enough, golden, sweet.

Synonym suggestions: lovely, cash, happiness, unseeing, sufficient, valuable, appealing.

Hitting the headlines. Writing activity.

Metaphors and similes

As easy as falling off a log. as light as a feather, as smooth as silk, as black as night, as solid as a rock, as white as a sheet, as hard as nails, as dry as a bone, as thin as a rake, as thick as two short planks, as old as the hills.

Setting the scene. Writing activity.

Metaphorically speaking. He was able to do anything he wanted; She looked everywhere; It was a shock; They were happy; It was devastating; He encountered a disturbance.

Not what they seem. build, burn, bite, laugh, jump, eat, rise, cry, fight, bury.

Only human. screaming, whispering, dancing, smiling, striding, gurgling.

Puns, riddles and crosswords

Riddle-me-re. Vocabulary.

Speaking of puns. drily, huskily, lightly, soundly, airily, meaningfully, weakly, aimlessly.

Name that pun. *Clifftop Tragedy* by Eileen Dover; *Great Floods of our Time* by Ivor Bucket; *The Rites of Spring* by Teresa Green; *Stormy Weather* by Gail Force; *Prison Memoirs* by Terry Bull; *Travelling Light* by Millie Pede.

Rebus. Dear Heidi, Thank you for stopping to talk to me today. I hate not having any time to see more of you. You make me happy. I hear you are having an expensive CD player for Christmas. What could be nicer. Excuse scribble. Billy.

Acrostic. Writing activity.

Word squares

```
B A T
A X E
T E N

C R A G S
R E L I C
A L I V E
G I V E N
S C E N E
```

Letter games. Children's choice.

Palindromes. mum, dad, noon, pop, pip, pup, deed, Bob, Hannah.

Pangrams. Children's choice.

Crossword clues. Children's choice.